So *That's* Where I Put That!

Humor
and light
reflections
for getting
through
those
senior
moments

So *That's* Where I Put That!
ISBN 978-0-9853005-7-9

Published by Product Concept Mfg., Inc.
2175 N. Academy Circle #200, Colorado Springs, CO 80909

Written and Compiled by Vicki Kuyper
in association with Product Concept Mfg., Inc.

All scripture quotations are from the King James version
of the Bible unless otherwise noted.

Scriptures taken from the Holy Bible,
New International Version®, NIV®.
Copyright © 1973, 1978, 1984 by Biblica, Inc.™
Used by permission of Zondervan.
All rights reserved worldwide.
www.zondervan.com

Sayings not having a credit listed are contributed by writers
for Product Concept Mfg., Inc. or in a rare case,
the author is unknown.

So *That's* Where I Put That!

Forgetfulness is the beginning of happiness
as fear is the beginning of wisdom.
Gabriel de Tarde

Dedicated to
Women of a Certain Age

We are women of vision. However, at our age that vision may require a pair of reading glasses. And unfortunately, after we put them on (if we can find them), we may totally forget what we were so intent on seeing more clearly in the first place.

If there's ever been a time in our lives when we don't want to misplace our sense of humor—this is it! So, hold onto your faith and your funny bone. Because, frankly, you'll never again be as young as you were the moment you started reading this book...

Carpe …Um?

As the years pass, we become more acutely aware of what a gift God gives us in each and every day. We strive to be intentional about how we spend the time we've been given. After all, we want to live life to the fullest! We want to Carpe the Diem—with all our heart! But, how are we supposed to seize the day when we can't even remember why we entered a room???

What did we come to seize? We open the fridge and look at the contents like they belong to someone else. Were we going to make eggs for breakfast? Maybe we were just grabbing a bottle of water… Or perhaps, we're still looking for our reading glasses and figure the fridge is as good of a place as any to start the search.

Yes, it's that time of life when our Carpe Diem has transformed into Carpe …Um? Sure, we can boost our caffeine intake, write ourselves a note as soon as we think of something we're going to do and hold onto it until we've actually accomplished the task, or simply get used to wandering around with a dazed look in our eyes. On the positive side, our aimless meandering counts toward our daily goal of 10,000 steps!

But, at its heart, Carpe Diem means making the most of what we have where we are right now. And right now, we're in a season where our brains go a bit foggy, sometimes. So, let's learn to lighten up a bit by laughing at ourselves, doing our level-headed best, and celebrating what we do remember! Let's live our lives in line with Psalm 118:24, "This is the day which the Lord hath made; we will rejoice and be glad in it." Let's not only Carpe Diem (Seize the Day), but Carpe Deus (Seize God) throughout each day. He's never absent, even when we're absent-minded.

The advantage of a bad memory
is that one enjoys several times the same good
things for the first time!

Friedrich Nietzsche

Three things happen as we age. First, the memory goes.
Then…I forget the other two.

One of the many things nobody ever tells you
about middle age is that it's such a nice change
from being young.
Dorothy Canfield Fisher

Old minds are like old horses;
you must exercise them if you wish to keep them
in working order.
John Adams

You don't stop laughing when you grow old,
you grow old when you stop laughing.
George Bernard Shaw

Age is an issue of mind over matter.
If you don't mind, it doesn't matter.
Mark Twain

There's Nothing Like an Old Friend

A group of long-time friends met at a different restaurant on the first Tuesday of every month for a little fun, food, and conversation. They were all talking about how wonderful the cannoli was at the restaurant where'd they'd met the previous month. All, except Lisa, who'd been out of town that week. "So, where'd you go?" Lisa asked.

Barb, the woman to her right, asked, "What's the name of that flower you give to someone you love? You know... The one that's red and has thorns."

"Rose?" Lisa replied.

"Yea, that's the one," Barb said. She turned to the woman on her right and said, "Hey, Rose, what's the name of that restaurant we went to last month?"

You know you're getting older...
when you see a cute guy and start to calculate if you could be his mom.

Clever Cat

A beleaguered police dispatcher received a phone call. "I've lost my cat" the woman cried, "and I need you to help me find her." The dispatcher sighed. "We really can't help you with that today, because…" "Oh, but you must," the woman interrupted. "You see, she's a really intelligent cat. She can even talk!" "Well then," the dispatcher said. "Perhaps we'd better hang up right now, because I'm sure she's trying to call you."

AEROBICS:
a series of strenuous
exercises that convert fats,
sugars, and starches into aches,
pains and chocolate cravings.

A show-off is any child more
talented than your own.

If children grew up according
to early indication,
we should have nothing
but geniuses.
Johann Wolfgang von Goethe

Our Birthday

Samuel W. Johnson

May this birthday fix in memory
the rich experiences of life;
Bring you closer friends and friendships,
dearer for the strife.

May good fortune travel with you,
bearing treasures all the way,
Not so plenteous as to spoil for you
the simple joys of every day.

May happiness long be yours to hold
as you go farther on your way,
With a smile of sincerity to meet you
and to greet you every day.

To Tell the Truth

When a woman called 911 complaining of difficulty breathing, the EMT rushed to her home. He placed a sensor on her finger to measure her pulse and blood oxygen. Then he began to gather her information. "What's your age?" he asked.

"Forty-six," answered the patient, eyeing the beeping device on her finger. "What does that do?"

"It's a lie detector," said the EMT with a straight face. "Now, what did you say your age was?"

"My mistake," the woman answered sheepishly, "I meant fifty-two."

You know you're getting older…
when you start lying about your childrens' ages.

Close Your Eyes and Make a Wish!

Where is the tipping point for birthdays? When do we stop rounding up when it comes to our age and start rounding down? As kids, we were proud of every single day we had under our belt. We weren't just five and a half. We were five years and seven months! We boasted about our age as though it were a milestone we'd worked incredibly hard to achieve.

Now, we're tempted to hide our age under our hat— or, at least, under a thick layer of liquid foundation. We're pleased, instead of perturbed, if someone guesses we're younger than the age on our driver's license. And even though we like parties, our birthday seems to be less of a party and more of a wake, lamenting the days gone by. If the truth be told, we're really just showing up for the cake. (Unless, of course, our aging body has forced us to go gluten-free. Then, we may as well eat our paper party hat and call it a day.)

But, if we look back—way back— to the day we were born, we realize that our current birthday isn't really all that different. There was lots of crying and confusion and bright lights back then, too. All we really wanted was some food, a dark womb, and a long nap.

We wanted to go back to the comfort of what we knew. But, look at us now! In the long run, life on the outside was definitely a step up—even though it seemed like a rather alarming change at the time.

The same thing can be true about getting older. Youth looks pretty inviting, because it's what we know. Or, knew. But, life on the other side of youth is just another invitation to change. Change is uncomfortable because it's unfamiliar, but that doesn't make it bad. Just different.

Why not anticipate the coming year with the same excitement we had as a kid? We have no idea what lies ahead! This could very well be the best year of our lives. New adventures, new friends, new insights…who knows the gifts this age will hold? So, when it comes time to blow out those candles, let's close our eyes and make a wish—for the courage to let go of the past and embrace whatever awaits us on the horizon of this brand new year.

Remember ye not the former things,
neither consider the things of old.
Behold, I will do a new thing; now it shall spring
forth; shall ye not know it? I will even make a way
in the wilderness, and rivers in the desert.
Isaiah 43:18-19

The Best of Intentions

A few days before her 40th birthday, Carl's wife mentioned how much she'd love to be ten again. So, on the big day, Carl made her a big stack of chocolate-chip pancakes, her childhood favorite. Then, he took her to the playground to feed the ducks. Next, they headed to the amusement park to ride the merry-go-round and eat snow cones.

That night, he served her a dinner of peanut butter and jelly sandwiches eaten in a fort made of blankets draped over the dining room table. This was followed by a cake with, "Happy 10th Birthday" written in frosting on the top.

Thoroughly pleased with himself, but aware that his wife had been kind of quiet throughout the day, Carl asked her, "So honey, did you enjoy being a kid for a day?"

His wife answered, "Thanks so much, but I meant a size 10."

You know you are older…
when your birthday candles
set off the smoke alarm.

There are three hundred and sixty-four days
when you might get un-birthday presents,
and only one for birthday presents, you know.
Lewis Carroll

Our birthdays are feathers
in the broad wing of time.
Jean Paul

A diplomat is a man who always remembers a
woman's birthday but never remembers her age.
Robert Frost

The belief that youth is the happiest time of life is
founded on a fallacy. The happiest person is the
person who thinks the most interesting thoughts,
and we grow happier as we grow older.

William Lyon Phelps

It All Adds Up!

In front of friends and family, the guest of honor slowly stands to address the crowd at her retirement home. Beulah announces to them with pride, "The day before yesterday I was only ninety-seven. Next year I will be 100!"

Thinking Beulah's mind has taken a turn for the worst, the nurse in residence gently grasps her hand and quietly asks, "Now, Beulah, how can that be?"

"Well," Beulah says, "Today is January 1st and my birthday was on December 31st. So, the day before yesterday I was 97, yesterday I was 98. This year on December 31, I will be 99 and next year, on the 31st, I will be 100!"

You know you're getting older...
when the cost of your candles
exceed that of your cake!

Actual "Senior Moments" Insurance Claims

I thought my window was down, but I found out it was up when I put my head through it.

Coming home, I drove into the wrong house and collided with a tree I didn't have.

Leaving home for work I drove out of my drive and straight into a bus; the bus was five minutes early.

I pulled away from the side of the road,
glanced at my mother-in-law,
and headed over the embankment.

I don't know who was to blame for the accident; I wasn't looking.

I didn't think the speed limit applied after midnight.

I bumped into a lamp-post that was obscured by human beings.

Keep Your Chin Up!

We all want to stay healthy as we get older. Rita was no exception. So, when she received a coupon in the mail for a free session with a personal trainer at her neighborhood gym, she decided to give it a try. She put on her yoga pants (which had seen many more grocery store runs than downward dogs) and tried to look as confident as possible as she entered the crowded gym.

Rita showed her coupon to the woman at the counter and was told to wait for Rolf, her trainer, in the exercise area. While she waited, Rita watched all of the younger, fit, twenty-somethings around her lifting weights, running on treadmill-like contraptions, and doing a series of stretches on giant blow-up balls. Rita decided she should warm up while waiting for Rolf, so she searched the room for a piece of equipment she actually knew how to use. Across from the check-in counter, Rita noticed a metal bar not in use. Gathering all of her strength, Rita managed to do two chin-ups before giving up and simply dangling, knees bent, like an exhausted chimpanzee.

Just then, Rolf walked over and introduced himself. Smiling politely, the buff young trainer said, "If you'll let go of the coat rack and follow me, we can get started."

You know you're getting older…
when you put on a bikini, head to the beach,
and a total stranger gives you a thumbs up and says,
"Good for you!"

Middle age is the time when a man is always
thinking that in a week or two
he will feel as good as ever.

Don Marquis

A merry heart doeth good like a medicine.

Proverbs 17:22

Be careful about reading health books.
Some fine day you'll die of a misprint.

Markus Herz

Lost: One Mind, Still Relatively Young

Our very own bodies are sending us a wake-up call. They're telling us we're no longer a proverbial spring chicken. How? Lately, when our minds begin to wander, they forget the way home. One minute we're having an intelligent, fully lucid conversation. The next, we're like a search engine that's lost its internet connection. That little circle is spinning and spinning, telling us something is happening. We're trying to reconnect. But, at this moment, the information we need is currently unavailable until further notice. Usually that "notice" happens in the middle of the night. We wake up and yell out the name of that great book that was right on the tip of our tongue at lunch, but couldn't find its way up to our brain—until now.

We can blame our memory lapse on a lack of sleep or caffeine. We can point an accusing finger at stress, an overbooked schedule, or late onset ADD. Or maybe, we've been giving people a piece of our mind for so long, that we're worried we haven't saved enough for ourselves. However, chances are that when we not only forget the name of the book we're currently reading, but the names of our children (or call them by the name of the poodle we owned as a teen), it's simply time to admit: the old gray matter, she ain't what she used to be.

We can try exercising our sluggish cerebrum by doing crossword puzzles and math games. We can try amping up our caffeine intake or adding ginkgo biloba to our vitamin regimen. We can do more aerobic exercise, to try and get more blood and oxygen to our lethargic, wheezing little brain cells. However, the most helpful thing we can do is give ourselves a break.

We aren't perfect. Never have been and never will be. Only God can lay claim to that description. So, when someone's face rings a bell, but your brain refuses to open the door that reveals their name, or when your car keys seem to be on the lam—again—just tell yourself that your mind is buffering. Just like those movies you download on TV where the sound hasn't quite caught up with the picture. Put your pride aside. Don't be too proud to say, "I'm so sorry, but I'm having a senior moment. What's your name again?" Chances are they may have forgotten yours, as well!

Ephesians 4:2 NIV reminds us to be humble, gentle, patient and to accept each other with love. As we strive to relate to others in this way, let's show ourselves the same courtesy. Let's be patient and accept the new stage of life we're in, senior moments and all, grateful for every day of life that's brought us this far.

Everybody makes mistakes.
That's why they put erasers on pencils!

Was That a Two-Minute Egg?

Recognized as one of the most brilliant and influential scientists of all time, Sir Isaac Newton is best known for his laws of gravitation. But, that doesn't mean he was immune from the occasional senior moment. One day, his maid happened upon him staring, dumbfounded, at a pot of water boiling on the stove. In the pot was his watch. In his hand, was an egg.

My thoughts ran a wool-gathering; and I did like the countryman, who looked for his ass while he was mounted on his back.

Miguel de Cervantes

Best Forgetful Friend

Welsh poet Dylan Thomas was the best man in his good friend Vernon Watkins' wedding. Or, at least, he was supposed to be. Right before the ceremony, the groom received an envelope from Thomas. Inside were two letters. The first inquired as to the name of the church where the wedding would be held, which Dylan had forgotten. The second letter apologized for forgetting to mail the first.

It's the Little Things

A few weeks after Rebecca's forty-third birthday, she received a gift she wasn't expecting: the news that she was pregnant. Although surprised, she and her husband were also delighted. Nine months later, Rebecca delivered a healthy baby girl without a single complication. To celebrate, her entire neighborhood put up banners to welcome the happy family home.

That afternoon, Rebecca's next door neighbor, Gretchen, dropped by to offer her congratulations, as well as the gift of a hand knit baby blanket for the new arrival. When Gretchen asked to see the baby, Rebecca said, "She's sleeping right now. Why don't you come in and have some tea and cookies?"

The neighbors talked for about an hour, before Gretchen glanced at her watch and realized she needed to head off shortly for a previous commitment. "Can I just sneak in and take a peek at the baby?" she asked.

"In just a bit," Rebecca answered, offering her another cup of tea.

Another fifteen minutes passed, and Gretchen was getting a bit anxious. "I'm really going to have to be heading out," she told Rebecca. "But I'd love to see the baby before I leave."

Rebecca said with a smile, "I'd love to show her to you, but I have to wait until she wakes up and starts to cry, so I can show her to you in all her glory!"

Prayer in Chester Cathedral
Cheshire, England

Give me good digestion, Lord,
And also something to digest;
Give me a healthy body, Lord,
With sense to keep it at its best.

Give me a healthy mind, good Lord,
To keep the good and pure in sight;
Which, seeing sin, is not appalled,
But finds a way to set it right.

Give me a mind that is not bored,
That does not whimper, whine or sigh;
Don't let me worry overmuch
About the fussy thing called "I."

Give me a sense of humor, Lord,
Give me the grace to see a joke;
To get some happiness from life,
And pass it on to other folk.

Absentminded...Literally

François-Marie Arouet, known by his nom de plume "Voltaire," was a brilliant writer, historian, and philosopher in 18th century France. He was so beloved by the French people that after his death in 1778, his heart and brain were removed and kept as national treasures. For years, the government and Voltaire's heirs fought over where the honored organs should be kept. During this time, Voltaire's brain was accidentally placed in a chest of drawers—and, along with other random pieces of furniture, was auctioned off to anonymous bidders. While Voltaire's heart remains in the Bibliothèque nationale de France (National Library of France), the location of his brain remains a mystery.

"God gave us the gift of life. It is up to us
to give ourselves the gift of living well."

"I have chosen to be happy, it's good for my health."

"If God did not exist, it would be
necessary to invent him."

"What most persons consider as virtue,
after 40 is simply the loss of energy."

"If God made us in his image, we have certainly
returned the compliment."

Nostalgia

After years of working across the country from where her family lives, Wendy finally receives the opportunity to transfer back to her very own hometown. Once she's settled in, it's time to find a new dentist. While perusing the list of local dentists covered by her insurance, she recognizes the name of a good looking guy from her graduating class in high school, a mere 30 years ago.

When the day of her appointment arrives, Wendy's disappointed when the dentist walks in. Obviously, she's made a mistake. He's bald, has a belly that could rival Santa, and seems much older. But, just to be sure, she asks if he went to the high school she attended.

"Why, yes!" he said. "I graduated in '75."

"Oh, my goodness," Wendy exclaims, "You were in my class!"

"Really!" he responds. "That's incredible! What subject did you teach?"

You know you're getting older when…
your investment in health insurance is finally
paying off.

There is no defense against adverse fortune which is
so effectual as an habitual sense of humor.

Thomas W. Higginson

Age imprints more wrinkles in the mind
than it does on the face.

Michel de Montaigne

Old age is like everything else.
To make a success of it, you've got to start young.

Theodore Roosevelt

While one finds company in himself
and his pursuits, he cannot feel old,
no matter what his years may be.

Amos Bronson Alcott

Beauty Treatment

Gone are the days when we grabbed anything in our closet to wear, dabbed on a bit of mascara and were good to go. These days if we want to venture outside in public. We have to carefully weigh our options as we weigh ourselves: Today, do we go with the fat pants or the skinny pants? Only the magnitude of our water retention knows for sure.

We schedule extra time to attend to our hair. Yes, we go on a scavenger hunt to unceremoniously yank the gray strands from our scalp, but we're also forced to search other areas of the face for those little sprouts if only we can see well enough to accomplish this task while wearing our reading glasses.

As for make-up, Kabuki dancers get by with less. Our moisturizing day cream, complete with sunscreen, is followed by eye cream, neck cream, make-up primer, a fresh coat of foundation, and a dusting of powder to hold it all in place. A full coat of body lacquer could serve the same purpose in half the time.

And even after we've plucked and primped and polished as best we can, one glance in the mirror reminds us that no matter what we do, we can't turn back the clock. So, what do we do instead? We try using others as our mirror. We live for their offhanded compliment… "That outfit makes you look so thin!" "Where did you get those cute shoes?" "Have you lost weight?" And then we compare our image with theirs.

But, we were created as individuals, not carbon copies. Trying to cram ourselves into a mold we were never designed to fit leads only to frustration and disappointment.

Right along with our brains, our bodies are going through a change. We can fight it, but it's a fight we're destined to lose. That doesn't mean it's time to give up and plant ourselves on the couch with a bag of chips balanced on our chest for the next forty years. It means that our routine for self-care is in need of an update.

We need more sleep, more exercise, and fewer calories. Let's dress for the size we are, not the size we were. Let's accept the bodies we have, being thankful for all of the things that still work, instead of bemoaning the fact that things don't work quite the same way as they did.

Beauty is found in the warmth of our smile, the heartiness of our laughter, and the generosity of our spirit. Being more attractive as we age means attracting others to us more easily, because we view them with compassion, instead of viewing them as competition.

At 20 we dress carefully, because we worry about what other people will think. At 40 we dress the way we want, despite what other people think. At 60 we realize they haven't been thinking about us at all.

Cover Girl

Flipping through the pages of a magazine one evening, Lynn came across an ad for hair color. It featured a beautiful young model with the reddish brown shade of hair Lynn thought would flatter her own coloring. Wanting a second opinion, she turned to her husband, who was watching a sporting event on TV.

"So, how do you think this color would look on a face with a few wrinkles?" she asked.

He looked at the picture, took the magazine out of Lynn's hands and ripped out the page. Then, he crumpled it up, flattened it out, looked at it again, and said, "Just great, hon!"

Wrinkles should merely indicate where
smiles have been.

Mark Twain

As we grow old, the beauty steals inward.
Ralph Waldo Emerson

When grace is joined with wrinkles
it is adorable. There is an unspeakable
dawn in happy old age.
Victor Hugo

Eight-year-old Lila loved to watch her mother
get ready for work in the morning.
One morning Lila asked her mother what she
was putting on her face.
"I'm putting on my wrinkle cream,"
her mother answered.
"Oh," Lila said, thoughtfully.
"I thought they were natural."

Let age, not envy,
draw wrinkles on thy cheeks.
Thomas Browne

Gone, But Not Forgotten

Mallory and Lynn had been friends for decades. So, when Mallory noticed that Lynn was wearing a new locket, she asked if there was a photo or memento of some sort inside.

"Why, yes there is," Lynn said. "Inside is a lock of my husband's hair."

"But, Robert's still alive!" Mallory responded, a puzzled look on her face.

"I know," Lynn replied. "But his hair is gone."

What do you call a group of rabbits walking backward, single file?
A receding hare line.

As We Get Older,
So Do Our Parents...

An elderly gentleman had been having serious hearing problems for a number of years. Finally, he went to an audiologist to see what could be done to help. Once he was fitted with a set of hearing aids, the man's hearing improved 100%.

A month later, the gentleman returned for his check-up.

"Your hearing is perfect," the doctor reported. "Your family must be really pleased that you can hear again."

The gentleman replied, "Oh, I haven't told my family yet. I decided to just sit around and listen to the conversations for awhile. I've changed my will three times!"

Age should not have its face lifted,
but it should rather teach the world to
admire wrinkles as the etchings of experience
and the firm line of character.
Clarence Day

Little Brandon was fascinated watching his
grandmother as she cleaned her dentures.
He watched carefully—his mouth wide open
in wonder—as she carefully removed them,
brushed and rinsed them, and them popped
them back in. "Cool, Grandma!"
Brandon said with enthusiasm.
"Now take off your arm!"

You know you're getting older…
when your friends compliment you
on your alligator shoes and you happen
to be barefoot.

To keep the heart unwrinkled,
to be hopeful, kindly, cheerful, reverent—
that is to triumph over old age.
Amos Bronson Alcott

Nobody grows old merely by living a number of years. We grow old by deserting our ideals. Years may wrinkle the skin, but to give up enthusiasm wrinkles the soul.

Samuel Ullman

At Sharon's weekly weight loss meeting, an older woman consistently lost more weight during the week than anyone else. "How do you do it?" Sharon asked, hoping for some tip she could follow. "Easy," the elderly woman said. "Every night I take my teeth out at six o'clock."

With mirth and laughter
let old wrinkles come.

William Shakespeare

Age encourages us to learn all kinds of new skills, such as special texting abbreviations in preparation for the senior years:

BFF: Best Friend Fainted

BYOT: Bring Your Own Teeth

FTW: Forgot the Word

FMM: Forgot My Meds

FWIW: Forgot Where I Was

CBM: Covered by Medicare

LMDO: Laughing My Dentures Out

TGIF: This Gal Is Forgetful

WAIT: Who Am I Texting?

BTW: Bring The Wheelchair

ROFL...CGU: Rolling On Floor Laughing...
Can't Get Up!

GGLKI: Gotta Go, Laxative Kicking In!

Failproof Password

With all of the accounts we use these days that require a password, it can be problematic remembering them all—especially as our brain nears menopause. Why not change it to "incorrect"? Then, anytime you log in with the wrong password, the computer will remind you, "Your password is incorrect."

Faulty Connection

While visiting her grandkids, Maggie wanted to connect her e-reader to their home's Wi-Fi. Naturally, she headed straight to her grandson's room for help.

"What's your family's Wi-Fi password?" Maggie asked 12-year-old, Grant.

Grant looked up from his homework and said, "It's taped under the modem." Then, he went back to studying for his algebra test.

Five minutes later, Maggie knocked timidly on Grant's door. "Sorry to bother you again, but I've tried three times and I still can't make it work. Am I spelling this right: T-A-P-E-D-U-N-D-E-R-T-H-E-M-O-D-E-M?"

It's All Geek to Me

There are few things that can make you feel as out-dated as a 5-year-old PC like having to ask your kids, or (before we know it!) their kids, how to navigate a new piece of technology. Whether it's downloading a new ringtone on your phone or uploading the latest software onto your tablet, knowing which button to click and when seems to be something that even a pre-schooler can master. So, why is it so tough for us?

We can console ourselves with the fact that our very own cell phone has more computer power than all of NASA had available back in 1969—when they successfully landed two men on the moon. But, some-how it seems that the bigger the hard drives and faster the internet speed we have available to us, the smaller our own brain power is and slower we are to catch on to what millenials seem to have hard-wired into their brains.

Let's be honest. We can't even remember our own passwords, let alone how to realign the wireless printer or operate the four remotes we need just to turn on the TV. But, just think about how much has changed since we were kids. TVs grew skinnier, while we expanded. Computers went from taking up entire rooms to residing on our desk, then our lap, then our phone (which moved from the wall into our pocket), and even onto our wrist. We have cars that can park themselves—and even drive themselves. We're living in a science fiction film from our youth!

But, some days, it feels more like a horror film. Just as we approach the age where we've gained a true appreciation for the joys of elastic waist pants and no make-up, video chatting comes into fashion. Now, we need to schedule an appointment with our hairstylist before we schedule a time to chat with our extended family. Of course, if we could take a decent selfie, we could stay in touch through social media. How kids can fit an entire group of their friends on the screen of their phone, while the only photo we can get is of our left eye and jiggly jowl remains a mystery. Apparently, the older we get the more our arms tend to resemble those of a T-Rex.

Yet, there is good news. If the internet goes down, we still have a life. We own books with actual pages, powered solely by our imaginations. We know how to play cards with an actual deck and bowl with a real ball, instead of a video controller. We know how to load real film into a camera. We could even manage to operate a typewriter or a phone with a dial on it, if push came to shove. While it's true that in this digital world, sometimes our mental computing system is as slow as old-fashioned dial-up, we can console ourselves with the fact that we aren't obsolete. We're vintage chic.

Cyber Space Cadets

"C'mon, Grandma, you've gotta try it!" Grace's teenage grandson pleaded. He had no idea how his grandmother could have lasted this long without ever having used the internet.

"Ok," Grace said, reluctantly. She sat down in front of the computer, put on her reading glasses, and asked, "So, what do I do?"

"Here," her grandson explained. "I'm opening the home page of the search engine. Now, you can type in any question you want into the bar over here and you'll find the answer to your question!"

Grace looked at her grandson, then back at the computer for a second, and then slowly began to type, "How is Gertrude doing this morning?"

You know you're getting older…
when you change your password to: GoofyHuey-
LouieDeweyDaisyDonaldMickeyMinniePhoenix,
because you were told it had to be at least eight
characters with one capital.

Even Really Smart Folks Have "Senior Moments"

The Climate Crasher

NASA's Climate Orbiter was designed to orbit Mars and study its surface. In 1999, after 286 days and 416 miles, the unmanned spacecraft finally reached its destination. However, the Orbiter didn't live up to its name. The reason? Its navigation system was designed by two separate teams, one in Colorado and one in California. One used the metric system, while the other used the American system of measurement which utilizes inches and feet. Neither checked the others' work. Obviously, the numbers didn't add up. Instead of orbiting the red planet, the spacecraft headed straight for the planet's surface and crashed.

Taxi, Please!

We pay homage to French physicist André-Marie Ampère every time we use the word "amp" (short for "ampere"), which is the measure of electric current. But, Ampère's work with electromagnetism sometimes overwhelmed his common sense. Ampère often kept a piece of chalk in his pocket, so when a problem he was working on in his head began to sort itself out, he could jot his revelatory equations down anywhere, anytime. That's precisely the scenario that led the physicist to begin scribbling equations on the back of a hansom cab one day as he was walking down the streets of Paris. Unfortunately, his solution disappeared when the cab left, taking his brilliant calculations with it.

One Thing at a Time

Work while you work,
Play while you play;
That is the way
To be cheerful and gay.

All that you do,
Do with your might;
Things done by halves
Are never done right.

One thing each time,
And that done well,
Is a very good rule,
As many can tell.

Moments are useless
Trifled away;
So work while you work,
And play while you play.

M. A. Stodart

You Know You're Getting Older…
When You Need Tech Support Even More Than Support Hose

After trying for hours to try and get her computer to do what she wanted it to do, Edith finally got up the courage to call Tech Support for help.

The young man on the end of the line told Edith to right-click on the Open Desktop.

"OK," Edith replied.

"Did you get a pop-up menu?" he asked.

"No," she said.

"OK," he said, patiently. "Right click again. Do you see a pop-up menu?"

Edith sighed. "No. Not yet."

The young tech support fellow was baffled. "OK, m'am, uh…Have you done something other than right click on your desktop?

"No," Edith replied. "You told me to Write 'click' and I wrote 'click.' Now what?"

I'm not young enough to know everything.
J. M. Barrie

Modern Signs of Friendship

You walk into her house and your WiFi
automatically connects.

Social media automatically tags photos
of you in her social media account.

You remember her birthday without
setting an alert on your phone.

You've shopped together so much that you own
several identical items of clothing—but before
wearing any of them, you text to make sure she
isn't wearing the same thing.

If she happens to be driving when you visit the
ATM, you trust her with your PIN number.

She has her own special ring on your cell phone.

You only post flattering photos of her online.

There is no friend like an old friend
Who has shared our morning days,
No greeting like his welcome,
No homage like his praise.
Frame is a scentless flower,
With gaudy crown of gold;
But friendship is the breathing rose,
With sweets in every fold.

Oliver Wendell Holmes

Always I have a chair for you in the smallest
parlor in the world, to wit, my heart.

Emily Dickinson

To your good health, old friend,
May you live for a thousand years,
And I be there to count them.

Robert Smith Surtees

I Dreamed a Dream

When you were a child, what did you dream of becoming when you grew up? A ballerina? A teacher? An astronaut? A wife and mother? A neurologist or archaeologist? Did that dream come true? Or did you learn to dream, and live, a new dream?

Just because we're grown-ups doesn't mean we're all grown up. Growing older means we're still growing, changing, becoming…someone different from who we are today. That means there's still time to dream, as well as time for those dreams to come true.

Sure, we may have to modify our dreams a bit. At forty-five, we're not going to become the principal ballerina for a major dance company, especially if we never got around to taking those ballet classes we always wanted to try. But, we can still dance! We can take a barre class or ballet class geared toward our age and experience. We can volunteer to help out where needed at a dance studio. We can dance while we do the dishes. We can watch a professional ballet company perform and live vicariously through the talent of others. We can connect with, and celebrate, the part of us that is awakened and inspired by the beauty of movement and music. There's more than one way to fulfill a dream.

As we get older, it's only natural for old dreams like these to bob to the surface of our psyche. We're becoming more aware that our time on this earth is limited—and that there's only so much we can pack into one lifetime. Also, our usually dependable bodies refuse to be pushed to the limits we may have successfully pushed when we were younger.

Now, staying up all night, eating cold pizza for breakfast, and trying to cram a lot of information into our brain right before being tested on it would undoubtedly result in disaster. And heartburn.

Reevaluating long held dreams in light of our current capabilities, commitments, and interests, is a good thing. When we do, we may find that some dreams we've been holding on to are purely for nostalgia's sake. Maybe the dream we had of skydiving at 18 has lost its appeal at 48. Maybe we'd rather spend the money hanging out at the spa. There's no shame in letting a dream die a timely death. Some dreams are merely whims tied up tightly with emotional ribbons.

But, as for those other dreams, the ones that continue to tug at our heart, maybe it's time to take a closer look. What is it about this particular aspiration that connects so deeply with you? What is it you're longing for? A sense of accomplishment? Fulfillment? Respect? Worth? Proof that your mature self is just as valuable, desirable, talented, strong, or adventurous, as you were when you were younger?

Sometimes, the dreams we hold on to, yet never seem to fulfill, are God-given longings in disguise. They're God's whisper, calling us to draw closer to Him and closer to becoming the woman He created us to be. Listen… What do your dreams have to say to you today?

So teach us to number our days, that we may apply our hearts unto wisdom.
Psalm 90:12

Dreams

Charlotte was in her late forties and still dreamed of one day becoming a writer. So, she went to God and prayed, "Dear, Lord, please help me become a great writer."

To her surprise, God answered aloud, asking, "How do you define 'great'?"

"I want to write things that the whole world will read," Charlotte said. "I want to write things that people will react to on a truly emotional level, things that will make them cry, that will lead them to the depths of anger and despair, which will then lead them to prayer."

"It will be so," God promised.

The following week, Charlotte was hired by a software company to write error messages.

When I was young I was amazed
at Plutarch's statement that the elder
Cato began at the age of eighty
to learn Greek. I am amazed no longer.
Old age is ready to undertake tasks
that youth shirked because
they would take too long.

W. Somerset Maugham

Pray as though everything
depended on God.
Work as though everything
depended on you.

Augustine of Hippo

Keep praying, but be thankful that God's
answers are wiser than your prayers!
William Culbertson

I have now spent fifty-five years in resolving:
having, from the earliest time almost that I can
remember, been forming plans for a better
life. I have done nothing. The need of doing,
therefore, is pressing, since the time of doing is
short. O GOD, grant me to resolve aright, and
to keep my resolutions, for Jesus Christ's sake.
Amen.
Samuel W. Johnson

It seems to me that we can never give up longing and wishing while we are thoroughly alive.
There are certain things we feel to be beautiful
and good, and we must hunger after them.
George Eliot

God's gifts put man's best dreams to shame.
Elizabeth Barrett Browning

What we truly and earnestly aspire to be, that
in some sense we are. The mere aspiration,
by changing the frame of the mind,
for the moment realizes itself.
Anna Brownell Jameson

Even Famous Writers Have "Senior Moments"

The Mystery of the Missing Sock

Reverend William Lisle Bowles was a friend of Great Britain's Lake Poets, which included such well-known writers as William Wordsworth and Samuel Taylor Coleridge. Though Bowles was himself a minor poet, he's remembered as much for his forgetfulness, as for his writing. One evening he was holding a dinner party for friends at his house. Although the guests had arrived, Bowles hadn't yet come down from upstairs. When his wife went up to see what was keeping him, she found him wearing one sock and frantically searching the bedroom for its mate. He admitted he'd been distracted thinking about a poem he was writing. His wife helped solve the mystery—he'd put both socks on the same foot.

I Knew I Liked That Author!

Leisurely browsing a bookstore one day, Scottish writer John Campbell became engrossed in a remarkable book. It wasn't until he'd purchased it, brought it home and read nearly half of it that he realized he'd written it.

Have regular hours for work and play; make each day both useful and pleasant, and prove that you understand the worth of time by employing it well. Then youth will be delightful, old age will bring few regrets, and life will become a beautiful success.

Louisa May Alcott

Rest is not idleness, and to lie sometimes on the grass under trees on a summer's day, listening to the murmur of the water, or watching the clouds float across the sky, is by no means a waste of time.

John Lubbock

It is vain for you to rise up early, to sit up late, to eat the bread of sorrows: for so he giveth his beloved sleep.

Psalm 127:2

All our life is a celebration for us; we are convinced, in fact, that God is always everywhere. We sing while we work, we sing hymns while we sail, we pray while we carry out all of life's other occupations.

Clement of Alexandria

Were it not for my little jokes, I could not bear the burdens of this office.

Abraham Lincoln

I asked God for strength, that I might achieve;
I was made weak, that I might learn humbly to obey.
I asked for health, that I might do greater things;
I was given infirmity, that I might do better things.
I asked for riches, that I might be happy;
I was given poverty, that I might be wise.
I asked for power, that I might have the praise of men;
I was given weakness,
that I might feel the need of God.
I asked for all things, that I might enjoy life;
I was given life, that I might enjoy all things.
I got nothing that I asked for,
but everything I hoped for.
Almost despite myself,
my unspoken prayers were answered.
I am among all men most richly blessed.

Prayer of an Unknown Confederate Soldier

Young at Heart.....
Older a Bit Farther South

Have you ever dreamed of owning beachfront property? Here's your chance! Okay, so that's not totally accurate. There's no refreshing body of water included in the deal. However, you do receive your very own personal Sahara that shows up rather unexpectedly, day or night. Recreational equipment is also included, if you count the mood swings.

Yes, it's that time of life discretely referred to as: The Change. Back in our mother's day, this was a subject women rarely broached in mixed company. One hundred years ago it was rarely talked about at all, mainly because most women didn't live long enough to see it through to the other side. Today, there's a good chance we'll live to see our 80s or 90s, and some of us will even celebrate birthdays as centenarians.

To help you make the transition from premenopausal to postmenopausal, you've got lots of options available to you today. There's also plenty of information (and empathy) available online, as well as from your own physician. With a little thought and planning, you can figure out how to host a going away party for your estrogen in the way that best suits your own personal needs.

But, whatever you choose, chances are you're still going to feel like you're stuck in a sauna, with PMS, for a decade or so. This is your new reality. But, think back…You've survived something like this before. During the transition from pre-teen to teen, your skin was changing—so you changed how you took care of it. The shape of your body was changing—so you changed your wardrobe to compensate. Back then, you recognized that even more big changes were on the horizon, so you planned for the future. And as for those mood swings, you tried (and so did everyone else!) to extend to yourself a little extra grace. Welcome to your second adolescence!

Every transition in life is a series of "hellos" and "good-byes." Yes, soon you'll be saying "good-bye" to taut underarms, but you'll be saying "hello" to no longer having to buy most feminine hygiene products. That means more money to spend on chocolate!

Life is a series of transitions. We can dread them and complain about them or we can prepare for them and welcome them in with open—albeit jiggly—arms! One thing we cannot do is stop them. From birth to death and beyond, change is our constant companion. That's what's so exciting about every new day—it's never the same as the day before. Each new dawn is a gift, inviting us to take hold of it and savor the moments it brings. And just like on TV, we receive a bonus gift, as well. Instead of a free set of Ginsu knives, each new day comes with the free gift of aging. Let's open it gratefully and learn to embrace it, playfully.

Today is not yesterday. We ourselves change. How then, can our works and thoughts, if they are always to be the fittest, continue always the same? Change, indeed, is painful, yet ever needful, and if memory have its force and worth, so also has hope.

Thomas Carlyle

We must always change, renew, rejuvenate ourselves, otherwise we harden.

Johann Wolfgang von Goethe

Wherever we are, it is but a stage on the way to somewhere else, and whatever we do, however well we do it, it is only a preparation to do something else that shall be different.

Robert Louis Stevenson

As for old age, embrace and love it. It abounds with pleasure if you know how to use it. The gradually declining years are among the sweetest in a man's life; and I maintain that even when they have reached the extreme limit, they have their pleasure still.

Seneca

Put a Ring On It

When Tina started menopause, her mood swings were so unpredictable that her husband, Ron, bought her a mood ring. Ron figured that way he could visually monitor when a bad mood was approaching. When Tina was in a good mood, Ron noticed that the ring turned green. When Tina was in a bad mood, he noticed it left a big red mark on his forehead. Being a wise man, Ron vowed that next time he'd buy Tina a diamond…

A bend in the road is not the end of the road, unless you fail to make the turn!

To exist is to change, to change is to mature, to mature is to go on creating oneself endlessly.

Henri Bergson

The Good News About Mid-Life

The good news about mid-life is we realize
the glass really is half full. The bad news is our
teeth will soon be floating in it.

The good news is the growth of hair on our legs slows
down, which gives us extra time to take care of our newly
acquired mustache.

The good news is that even though our
memory is starting to go, we can still retain
some things: like water.

The good news is that we no longer have upper arms;
we have bonafide wingspans.

The good news is we become more interested
about getting in touch with our inner child.
The bad news is we have to travel through so
much more cellulite to find her.

The first 40 years of childhood are the hardest.
Author Unknown

Our days are a kaleidoscope. Every instant a change takes place… New harmonies, new contrasts, new combinations of every sort… The most familiar people stand each moment in some new relation to each other, to their work, to surrounding objects.
Henry Ward Beecher

Change is the nursery of music, joy, life and eternity.
John Donne

All changes, even the most longed for, have their melancholy, for what we leave behind us is a part of ourselves; we must die to one life before we can enter into another.
Anatole France

If wrinkles simply indicate "where smiles have been," my underarms must be incredibly jovial.

Lessons From Life

Watch the scenes along life's highways,
Study man a found in byways,
Struggling toward some loved goal.
These are lessons far more reaching
Than any philosophic teaching,
More of life and more of soul.

Look at man where you may find him,
Judge the future by the life behind him,
See all the footsteps come and go;
Of the beggar worn and weary,
Or some traveler, tired and dreary,
Reaping harvest of all they sow.

Study age with wisdom, gaze at beauty
Mark how few called are fit for duty
In the service of the world;
Learn the lessons from their stumbling,
Listen to the great world rumbling
With flags of war unfurled.

Grander than the books of sages
Are lessons written on nature's pages,
Read them over day by day;
Those are things that give us learning,
A thousand fold their good returning
To guide our feet along the way.

Samuel W. Johnson

Lose Yourself

At this stage of our lives, it's incredibly easy to lose our car keys, our reading glasses, our train of thought, or the elasticity in our skin. But, have you ever lost yourself—in a good way? Have you been so awestruck by a sunset that all the cares of the day seem to fade away? Have you ever lost track of time talking to dear friends way-too-late into the early morning hours? Have you ever been so lost in the music that you don't care who's watching you dance? When was the last time you sat quietly, just watching the world go by, without checking for messages or email on your phone?

Getting lost in thought is totally different than losing your train of thought. It's being so engaged in what you're experiencing that you forget about your To Do list, what you're wearing, what other people may be thinking, or the fact that you're getting older. It's times like these when your mind travels roads it may not otherwise explore. These roads can help you get in touch with what you love most about life—and about yourself. They can quiet your heart to the point where you know for certain that God is near.

So, how do we lose ourselves on purpose? The easiest way is to climb out of our daily ruts. That's easier said than done. We like what's familiar. We like to drive down the same street to work, shop at the same grocery store, hang out with the same friends, and head to our favorite vacation spot year after year. There's less stress when we refuse to push the boundaries of what's familiar, but there's also less awe. A mind set on auto-pilot is unlikely to veer off its well-worn path.

The longer we remain in the same rut, the deeper it gets, and the harder it is to change course. After awhile, the rut is so deep we can't even see over the sides. It feels risky, even downright dangerous, to choose the unknown. But, maybe it's time. Maybe that's exactly what we need to help us move into this next stage of life with a sense of adventure. Maybe it isn't getting older that's getting us down. Maybe we're just feeling bored. Bored with the prospect of the rest of our life looking exactly like today. Bored with being the same person tomorrow that we were yesterday.

Why not shake things up a bit? Starting today. Take a new route home from work. Turn off the TV and pick up a book. Start that diet, or exercise program, you've been putting off. Take a walk around the block, listening to the birds, instead of headphones. Plan a vacation to somewhere you've never been—maybe somewhere that requires a passport.

Then, sit quietly and talk to God about what doing something new has stirred up in you. But, don't stop there. Tomorrow's another day, another adventure, another chance to discover there's so much more to life—and you—than meets the eye.

Twenty years from now you will be more
disappointed by the things you didn't do
than by the ones you did do. So throw off the
bowlines, sail away from the safe harbor.
Catch the trade winds in your sails.
Explore. Dream. Discover.
Mark Twain

The real voyage of discovery consists not in seeking
new landscapes, but in having new eyes.
Marcel Proust

The person who has lived the most is not the one
with the most years
but the one with the richest experiences.
Jean Jacques Rousseau

Though we travel the world over to find the beautiful,
we must carry it with us, or we find it not.
Ralph Waldo Emerson

Not until we are lost do we begin to
understand ourselves.
Henry David Thoreau

Cited for Multi-tasking

An older woman was off on a road trip to visit her grandchildren. Unfortunately, as she was driving down the freeway she was 15 miles over the speed limit. A highway patrolman who happened to be in the lane to her left, pulls up next to her and glances over to assess the situation. That's when he sees that the woman is knitting, as she drives.

The patrolman slows his car a bit, falls back behind her vehicle, and turns on his lights. But, the woman doesn't pull over. Next, he turns on his siren. The knitting driver continues on down the highway, apparently oblivious to the fact that the patrolman is even there.

The patrolman tries once more to get the woman's attention. He pulls his car back up next to hers, cranks down the window, and yells through a bullhorn, "PULL OVER!"

"No," the old woman shouts back. "It's a scarf!"

You know you're getting older…
when you begin to see speed limits as a goal,
instead of a challenge.

"Senior Moments" From Around the World

Watch That First Step

In the 1930s, the leader of Greece, General George Metaxas, was inspecting one of the country's air bases. Asked if he wanted to try piloting a seaplane, the General answered with an enthusiastic, "Yes!" After a perfect flight, the Commander accompanying Metaxas noticed that the General was preparing to land the seaplane on the runway. As tactfully as possible, the Commander reminded the General that since the plane was really a flying boat, that it might be better to land it on the water. Metaxas apologized for his error and executed a perfect water landing. Then he rose from his seat, thanked the Commander for the experience, opened the door and fell into the sea.

I have found out that there ain't no surer way to find out whether you like people or hate them than to travel with them.

Mark Twain

It's not the road ahead that wears you out.
It's the grain of sand in your shoe.
Arabian Proverb

Never criticize a man until you've walked
a mile in his moccasins
Native American Proverb

Glorious it is when wandering time has come.
Eskimo Proverb

Travel, in the younger sort, is a part of education;
in the elder, a part of experience.
Francis Bacon

W.C. Fields was so worried about winding up in a
strange city without ample funds, that he opened
a bank account in every town he visited.
But he was also so worried about being robbed
that he used a different name for each account.
Unfortunately, because he never bothered to
write the names down he eventually
forgot all but 23—out of 700.

The journey of a thousand miles begins with
a single cash advance...

Memory is the diary we all carry about with us.
Oscar Wilde

I shall be telling this with a sigh somewhere ages
and ages hence: Two roads diverged in a wood,
and I—I took the one less traveled by,
and that has made all the difference.
Robert Frost

Adventure is worthwhile in itself.
Amelia Earhart

None are so old as those who have outlived
enthusiasm.
Henry David Thoreau

The important thing is this: to be able at any moment
to sacrifice what we are for what we could become.
Charles Du Bos

Warning: Road Construction Ahead

Life may be an adventure, but along the road there are plenty of potholes, detours, and dead-ends that get in the way of what we view as progress. Some of them are inconvenient. Some are uncomfortable. Some are totally heartbreaking. And the older we get, the less quickly we seem to bounce back to that point where we feel life is back to "normal."

Maybe that's just another part of growing up as we grow older: realizing that "normal" a moving target. Today will never be exactly the same as tomorrow, or yesterday. Change happens. And sometimes it happens in the blink of an eye. So, when life bounces us right out of our momentary "normal" onto an unfamiliar road, it's time to stop looking in the rear view mirror. We can't change the past and we have no control over the future. The only moment we can do anything about is right now.

So, what will we do? Moan, groan, and drag our feet every step of the way? Dig in our heels and refuse to move forward at all? Or, will we take a deep breath, gather up what we know about God and ourselves, and then move forward with hopeful anticipation, instead of trepidation? The way we choose to proceed will make all the difference in whether we look forward to the future or spend the rest of our lives longing for the "good old days."

When life turns upside-down, stop and remember when topsy-turvy times have brought unexpected blessings. That dreaded cross country move that led you to cross paths with your best friend for life… The restaurant that was closed that forced you to try somewhere new, which turned out to be one of your most memorable meals ever… That chance meeting that introduced you to your future spouse… The job that you lost that led to the job that you loved…

We cannot see the end of the road from where we stand right now. And that's a blessing. If we knew in advance how hard some things in our future would be, we might choose to bypass them by going another way—and we'd miss out on some amazing adventures we couldn't experience any other way. Just imagine if our fear of going through labor prevented us from ever having children. We'd miss out on one of the greatest joys of life.

We may view middle age itself as a pothole, detour, or dead-end. We may feel that this whole aging thing is robbing us of the joy we experienced when we were younger, fitter, faster on our feet and in our mind. But joy, just like "normal," isn't something static. It ebbs and flows like the sea, uncovering new treasures with the power of each brand new wave. There are places we've never been, friends we've not yet met, sights we've never seen, and insights we haven't yet experienced enough to understand, all waiting for us down the road. It may be a bumpy ride at times, but life is a journey that can only be appreciated when we finally come to the end of the road. Today, we've still got a ways to travel.

The block of granite which is an obstacle in the
pathway of the weak, becomes a stepping-stone
in the pathway of the strong.
Thomas Carlyle

Difficulties are not a passing condition that we must
allow to blow over like a storm so that we can set
to work when calm returns.
They are the normal condition.
Charles de Foucauld

No longer forward nor behind I look in hope or fear;
but grateful, take the good I find,
the best of now and here.
John Greenleaf Whittier

It has done me good to be somewhat parched by the
heat and drenched by the rain of life.
Henry Wadsworth Longfellow

> An adventure is only an inconvenience
> rightly considered. An inconvenience is only
> an adventure wrongly considered.
>
> G. K. Chesterton

British author G. K. Chesterton, was renowned for being rather absent-minded. One time, he was at the train station, walked up to the ticket window, and ordered a cup of coffee. He was promptly directed to the restaurant. Once there, he successfully ordered his coffee and sat down to wait for his train—and tried to buy his ticket from the waiter.

Another time, G. K. Chesterton knew he was late for a very important appointment. But, as he was hurrying down the street, he passed the local dairy he'd often visited as a child. Feeling thirsty, he stopped in for a glass of milk. Then, he happened to pass a gun shop. Since he'd been meaning to buy a firearm for quite awhile, he stopped in and carefully made a purchase. Only then did it dawn on him that the important engagement he was rushing to was his own wedding.

There is in every true woman's heart a spark
of heavenly fire, which lies dormant in the broad
daylight of prosperity; but which kindles up,
and beams and blazes in the dark hour of adversity.
Washington Irving

Troubles are often the tools by which God
fashions us for other things.
Henry Ward Beecher

'Tis easy enough to be pleasant,
When life flows along like a song;
But the man worth while
is the one who will smile
When everything goes dead wrong.
Ella Wheeler Wilcox

Rebellion against your handicaps gets you nowhere.
Self-pity gets you nowhere. One must have the
adventurous daring to accept oneself as a bundle of
possibilities and undertake the most interesting game
in the world—making the most of one's best.
Harry Emerson Fosdick

God hath not promised
Skies always blue,
Flower-strewn pathways
All our lives through;
God hath not promised
Sun without rain,
Joy without sorrow,
Peace without pain.
But God hath promised
Strength for the day,
Rest for the labor,
Light for the way,
Grace for the trials,
Help from above,
Unfailing sympathy,
Undying love.

Annie Johnson Flint

More "Senior Moments" From Around the World

At fifty, I take great comfort in God. I think He is considerably amused with us sometimes.

James Russell Lowell

Not-So-Handy Man

In Cannes, France, in 1985, doctors were astounded when they saw the image of a 7-inch screwdriver in the x-ray of a man's head. The man had been complaining of headaches, so they assumed the man must have suffered a horrific accident. However, on further examination, they realized the screwdriver wasn't actually in the man's head, but had been left in the x-ray machine by a technician.

"I Need a Longer Extention Cord..."

In 1890, Abyssinian emperor Menelik II decided to take steps toward modernizing his kingdom of Ethiopia. So, he ordered the latest advance in criminal justice from New York City: three electric chairs. Apparently, the emperor was unclear on the fact that they needed electricity to work, which was not available in Ethiopia at the time. Consequently, two of the chairs were quickly disposed of. The third, however, made a very modern-looking emperor's throne.

Second Thoughts

When Sarah's mother became increasingly forgetful, Sarah knew it was time to help move her into an assisted living facility. So, she set up a tour of the one with the highest recommendations in town.

When Sarah met with the director, she admitted, "I'm really uncertain about this decision. How do you determine whether someone is ready to move in?"

"Well," the director said, "we fill a bathtub. Then, we offer a teaspoon, a teacup, and a bucket to the potential client and ask him or her to empty the bathtub."

"Oh, I understand," Sarah said. "A person who still has all of their mental faculties would use the bucket, because it's bigger than the spoon or the teacup."

"No," the director replied. "A normal person would pull the plug. Would you like a bed near the window or the dining room?"

You know you're getting older…
when you spot that first gray hair—on your kid.

When The Joke's On You....

If you've ever envied people who seem to be natural comedians and wished that you, too, were blessed with the gift of making others laugh—here's your chance. You're entering a phase of life where every day you discover that the joke is on you! A simple distraction while getting ready for work means you arrive with make-up completed on only one eye. After complaining to the bank teller that the ATM isn't accepting your pin code, it dawns on you that you've been entering your gate code for the last five minutes. An all-out search for your reading glasses ends badly when your spouse points out they're perched right on top of your head.

Scenarios like these begin to happen so frequently that you start looking for the hidden camera, hoping you've been set up, instead of fearing you're losing your faculties. Welcome to the "forgetful years." They're kind of like training wheels, getting you ready to maneuver the full-fledged "senior moments" which await you a little farther down the road. These little farcical faux-pas are more than annoyances or embarrassments. They're actually valuable teachers— because, if we haven't learned to laugh at ourselves by now, we're running out of time.

Taking ourselves lightly becomes increasingly more helpful as we age. As we become more dependent on others, when our bodily functions become a topic discussed around the dinner table, and our brain seems to go out as frequently as our trick knee, being able to laugh at ourselves will put those helping us at ease. It will do the same for us. Learning to laugh openly about an uncomfortable situation is always a better solution than trying to sweep our mistakes and missteps under the rug. It encourages others to be real with us, in the same way that we're being real with them. It reminds us all that there are plenty of things in this world worth being serious about. Our personal pride is not one of them.

Exercising your funny bone now will help get you in shape to use it effectively later. So, if you happen to find your credit card in the vegetable crisper, forget trying to pass the blame onto the dog. Feel free to roll your eyes at yourself, have a good laugh, and then share your "middle-aged moment" with a friend. She may have one of her own she now feels comfortable enough to share with you.

Someone's Occu-pewing My Pie!

Born in 1844, William Archibald Spooner was by all accounts a brilliant young man. He received a scholarship to New College, Oxford, where he earned degrees in the Classics and Humanities, as well as a Doctorate in Divinity. Spooner remained at New College for the rest of his life as a lecturer, dean, and eventually warden (president) of the college.

But, Dr. Spooner isn't remembered for his work as an Anglican priest, scholar, or writer. Instead, his name lives on in what we call "spoonerisms." These are slips of the tongue where a person transposes the first letters or sounds of an adjoining word. For instance, you'd be making a spoonerism if you said (like the Reverend once did), "The Lord is a shoving leopard" when you actually meant, "The Lord is a loving shepherd." Apparently, the more excited or agitated Dr. Spooner was, the more prone to "spoonerisms" he became.

Often absent-minded, as well as tongue-tied, Spooner once ended a homily by saying, "In the sermon I just preached, whenever I said Aristotle, I meant Paul."

Here are just a few examples of Rev. Spooner's greatest gaffes, as recorded by former students and colleagues:

Paying a visit to the college dean, he reportedly asked, "Is the bean dizzy?"

On one occasion, Rev. Spooner said in a speech to Queen Victoria, "I have in my bosom a half-warmed fish" (that would be a "half-formed wish").

Once upon entering church, Spooner exclaimed to a woman who was in his seat, "Pardon me, but you are occu-pewing my pie!"

He once referred to a well-oiled bicycle as "a well-boiled icicle."

Getting totally tongue-tied one day when he dropped his hat, he reportedly asked, "Will nobody pat my hiccup?" ("that would be, "…pick up my hat!")

A man without mirth is like a wagon
without springs. He is jolted disagreeably
by every pebble in the road.
Henry Ward Beecher

I have always noticed that deeply and truly
religious persons are fond of a joke,
and I am suspicious of those who aren't.
Alfred North Whitehead

A sense of humor is a sense of proportion.
Kahlil Gibran

For health and the constant enjoyment of life,
give me a keen and ever present sense of humor;
it is the next best thing to an
abiding faith in providence.
George B. Cheever

God is the creator of laughter that is good.
Philo

Illuminating Check-Up

Mrs. Whitaker accompanied her husband of sixty years to his annual physical. When he was called in, she remained in the waiting room, leisurely enjoying a magazine.

Meanwhile, back in the exam room, Mr. Whitaker's check-up had gone without a hitch. "You're in amazing shape for your age!" his doctor commented. "How do you do it?"

"Well," said Mr. Whitaker, "I don't drink, I don't smoke, and the good Lord looks out for me. For weeks now, every time I go to the bathroom in the middle of the night, He turns the light on for me!"

Concerned over his patient's response, the doctor finds Mrs. Whitaker in the waiting room and tells her what her husband said.

"I don't think that's anything to worry about," she says. "And on the bright side, it does explain who's been peeing in the fridge."

You know you're getting older…
when the light at the end of the tunnel is the candles on your birthday cake.

The human race has only one really effective
weapon and that is laughter.
Mark Twain

It is the heart that is unsure of its God
that is afraid to laugh.
George MacDonald

I know not all that may be coming,
but be it what it will, I'll go to it laughing.
Herman Melville

He that is of a merry heart
hath a continual feast.
Proverbs 15:15

Sunshine and Music

A laugh is just like sunshine.
It freshens all the day,
It tips the peak of life with light,
And drives the clouds away.
The soul grows glad that hears it
And feels its courage strong.
A laugh is just like sunshine
For cheering folks along.

A laugh is just like music.
It lingers in the heart,
And where its melody is heard
The ills of life depart;
And happy thoughts come crowding
Its joyful notes to greet:
A laugh is just like music
For making living sweet.

Author Unknown

Go Ahead...Take the Cake

Let's talk cravings. Not since pregnancy, has there been a time in our lives when we crave carbs, sugar, and fat, more than during the premenopausal years. Since our minds are already in the pantry, regardless of where we're seated right now, let's go one step farther. Let's talk cake. Not the stuff that's been sitting on the grocery store shelf for three days, we're talking really GOOD cake...mile high, baked from scratch, layered with fluffy frosting (yet light-as-a-feather), culinary confection perfection.

It takes time and attention to bake a cake worthy of expectations like these. Not only do the ingredients have to be measured accurately, the cakes have to be cooled completely before being stacked one on top of the other. But, before the layering begins, the baker has to make certain that each layer can stand on its own. They can't have fallen in the middle or be cracked, crumbling, or broken into pieces. If they are, the cake will end up a lop-sided mess.

Of course, in our present situation we may not care if our cake resembles a cobbler. We'll eat it with a spoon, if need be. But, the same principles that make for assembling a successful layer cake, can also apply to building a successful life. If our foundation is crumbling, it isn't strong enough to hold anything substantial, or new, we try to build on top of it. Something's always going to come crashing down.

Our past is a foundation that's always with us. If it's been a rocky one, that doesn't mean it's an unsuitable foundation for a solid future. It simply means we need to make certain the rubble is cleaned away before we build something new. Grudges, lies, broken relationships, and emotional wounds can't be plastered over with time and a smile. They need to be acknowledged and dealt with in a godly way. That may involve facing some hard truths and tackling issues such as forgiveness, repentance, or reconciliation.

With God's help and, if needed, the help of a counselor or mentor, there's no rock so big that it cannot be broken into manageable-sized bits. Then, the remaining rubble can be carefully, and prayerfully, cleared away. This clean sweep helps you build a more emotionally secure future, one strong enough to hold the weight of decades of growth and change— one ready to be embellished with all the colors of joy.

Let us not clutter up today with the leavings
of other days.
Oliver Wendell Holmes

I have learned that success is to be measured
not so much by the position that one has reached in
life as by the obstacles which he has
overcome while trying to succeed.
Booker T. Washington

Regret is an appalling waste of energy; you can't
build on it; it is good only for wallowing in.
Katherine Mansfield

Forgiveness is the answer to the child's dream of
a miracle by which what is broken is made whole
again, what is soiled is made clean again.
Dag Hammarskjöld

We wish to preserve the fire of the past,
not the ashes.
William James

Ooops.....

To celebrate her 40th birthday, Lynette decided to buy a convertible sports car, along with a vanity license plate that read "18 Again." Lynette was pretty proud of her new ride and parked it directly in front of the dry cleaners where she was picking up her laundry, totally oblivious to the fact that she'd parked in a Deliveries Only spot. Not more than a minute later, a delivery truck driver walked into the dry cleaners and said, "Who owns the car with the plate, 'I ate again'?"

You know you're getting older…
when you speed because you don't want to forget where you're going.

Each part of life has its own pleasures.
Each has its own abundance harvest,
to be garnered in season...Life may be short,
but it is long enough to live honorably and well.
Old age is the consummation of life,
rich in blessings.

Cicero

To be seventy years young is
sometimes far more cheerful and hopeful
than to be forty years old.

Oliver Wendell Holmes

Be bold while you are young and stay young
while you are old.

Chinese Proverb

If youth only knew; if age only could.

Henri Estienne

Bless You!

In the middle of a live stage performance, a theater usher was alarmed to see an elderly woman crawling on her hands and knees beneath a row of seats in the balcony. He hurried to her side and whispered, "Excuse me, ma'am! You're disturbing the audience. Can I help you with something?"

She replied, "I'm so sorry, but I sneezed and lost my gum." Then, she continued her search.

"Ma'am," the usher said rather firmly, "if that's your only problem, allow me to get you some gum from the concession stand. Then you can return to your seat and enjoy the play. Certainly a stick of gum isn't worth all of this commotion."

"But, you don't understand," the woman said. "My false teeth are in it."

You know you're getting older…
when you stop searching for the meaning of life
to focus on searching for your car keys.

Redneck In The City

A redneck and his son went into the city for the first time. They walked inside a skyscraper and stood in the lobby, watching as two metal doors parted and a work-worn elderly woman entered. The doors closed behind her. A few minutes later, the metal doors parted again, and a lovely young woman stepped out.

"You stay here, son," the man said. "I'm going home to fetch your mother and see if she'll get in that machine."

When everything seems to
be going against you,
remember that the airplane takes off
against the wind, not with it.
Henry Ford

Good-humor makes all things tolerable.
Henry Ward Beecher

Mountains are removed by
first shoveling away the small stones.

He hath made everything beautiful
in his time.
Ecclesiastes 3:11

New Eyes for Old Friends

We've reached that stage of life when the term "old friends" feels more literal every day. Instead of giggling together over a cute boy in class, we're now guffawing over our latest absent-minded mishap. We're discussing high fiber as often as high fashion, managing caregiving options for our parents instead of our kids, and trying to pinpoint the time when restaurants decided to make the print on their menus so incredibly small.

The good news is that one of the very best parts of aging is that our relationships grow up right along with us. Whether it's a friend, our spouse, or even our kids, those we love grow older, and hopefully wiser, right along with us. Every day we spend together adds another memory to the scrapbook of our lives.

But, there's a catch. The longer we know someone, the easier it is for us to take that person for granted. We feel so comfortable in their presence that we no longer strive to put our best foot forward. At times, our familiarity may even lead us to act like a heel. We're less careful with our words, and actions, than we would be with a new acquaintance. After all, we don't have to make a good impression. This person loves us for who we are, warts and all. While that may be true, it doesn't mean we should become so careless as to put that love to the test.

Love doesn't have a finish line. It's a lifelong pursuit. In any relationship, whether it's with a friend we've known since childhood or a spouse we've been married to for decades, we'll never have everything figured out. Let's face it, we've lived with ourselves 24/7 for our entire lives and we're still discovering more about who we are every single day. How can we possibly think we really "know" someone else?

That means every time we get together is a fresh opportunity to look at those we love with new eyes. If we were meeting them for the very first time, what would we appreciate about them most? What would we want to know more about? What can we learn from their unique life experience and point of view?

Instead of casually slipping back into the same conversations over and over again, let's stir up the relational pot. Let's ask questions intended to uncover more about the hearts of those we love and worry less about voicing our own stories and opinions. Let's focus on their strengths, instead of pointing out their faults. Let's give them the best of ourselves every time we're together. Let's consider the wonderful ways in which they've grown since we first met—and express to them just how blessed we are to have them in our lives.

A friend loveth at all times.
Proverbs 17:17

If you would be loved, love and be lovable.
Benjamin Franklin

It is a splendid thing to think that the woman you really love will never grow old to you. Through the wrinkles of time, through the mask of years, if you really love her, you will always see the face you loved and won. And a woman who really loves a man does not see that he grows old; he is not decrepit to her; he does not tremble; he is not old; she always sees the same gallant gentleman who won her hand and heart. I like to think of it in that way; I like to think that love is eternal. And to love in that way and then go down the hill of life together, and as you go down, hear, perhaps, the laughter of grandchildren, while the birds of joy and love sing once more in the leafless branches of the tree of age.
Robert G. Ingersoll

Those who love deeply never grow old; they may die of old age, but they die young.
Dorothy Canfield Fisher

Happily Ever After

Bob and Dorothy, both age 89, were over the moon about getting married. While they were out for their evening walk, discussing plans for their upcoming nuptials, they passed a drugstore.

"Hold on a minute," Bob said. "I want to speak to the pharmacist."

So, they went inside. They made their way to the back of the store, where Bob asked the pharmacist on duty, "Do you carry heart medication?"

"Naturally," the pharmacist replied.

"Medicine for rheumatism?" Bob queried.

"Absolutely," he said.

"Medicine for memory problems, arthritis and jaundice?"

The pharmacist puzzled a moment, then replied, "Of course…"

"How about vitamins, sleeping pills, iron supplements, and antacids?"

"Yes, but…"

"Do you sell wheelchairs and walkers?" Bob continued.

"All speeds and sizes," said the pharmacist with a sigh.

"Great!" Bob replied. "We'd like to register for our wedding gifts, please."

Happy Hearts

"I'll bet you don't know what day this is," the woman told her husband of many years. "Of course I do," he answered as he headed out the door. During the day, a bouquet of flowers, an elegant box of chocolates, and a gift card for her favorite dress shop were delivered to the home.

The woman couldn't wait to greet her husband at the door that evening. "Honey, thank you for the flowers, the chocolates, the gift card...I've never had a more wonderful Groundhog Day in all my life!"

The age of a woman doesn't
mean a thing. The best tunes are
played on the oldest fiddles.

Ralph Waldo Emerson

Oh, the comfort—
The inexpressible comfort of
feeling safe with a person—
having neither to weigh thoughts,
nor measure words, but pouring them
all right out, just as they are,
chaff and grain together;
certain that a faithful hand will
take and sift them,
keep what is worth keeping,
and then with the breath of kindness
blow the rest away.

Dinah Maria Craik

From quiet homes and first beginnings,
Out to the undiscovered ends,
There's nothing worth the wear of winning,
But the laughter and the love of friends.

Hilaire Belloc

A day for toil, an hour for sport,
but for a friend is life too short.

Ralph Waldo Emerson

I count myself in nothing else so happy
as in a soul remembering my good friends.

William Shakespeare

Forwarding Address: Heaven

Charlotte's best friend, Karen, was moving her small boutique across town to a larger, more centrally-located property. Wanting to acknowledge her friend's success, Charlotte decided to have a bouquet of flowers delivered to celebrate the Grand Opening.

By the time Charlotte arrived, the festivities were already in full swing. She headed to the back of the store, past the jewelry, knickknacks, and handmade pottery, to grab a refreshment. That's when Charlotte noticed that she wasn't the only one who'd had the idea to honor Karen with flowers. She glanced at the cards, wondering which bouquet was hers. She found a large arrangement of roses, holding a card signed with her name, but the message that accompanied the arrangement read, "Rest In Peace."

Upset and embarrassed over the florist's mistake, Charlotte headed back to the flower shop to complain. Upon hearing what had happened, the florist explained that Charlotte's bouquet had been switched with another customer's.

"I take full responsibility," he said. "We're so sorry for the mistake!"

"So, what are you going to do about it?" Charlotte asked, obviously annoyed.

"We'll provide a full refund, of course," the florist replied. Then, he continued, "But, there's no need to get upset. Look at the positive side! Somewhere, a funeral is taking place and they have a lovely floral spray with a note that says, 'Congratulations on your new location!'"

I shot an arrow into the air,
It fell to earth, I knew not where;
For, so swiftly it flew, the sight
Could not follow it in its flight.

I breathed a song into the air,
It fell to earth, I knew not where;
For who has sight so keen and strong,
That is can follow the flight of song?

Long, long afterward, in an oak
I found the arrow, still unbroke;
And the song, from beginning to end,
I found again in the heart of a friend.

Henry Wadsworth Longfellow

I want a warm and faithful friend,
To cheer the adverse hour;
Who ne'er to flatter will descend,
Nor bend the knee to power,
A friend to chide me when I'm wrong,
My inmost soul to see,
And that my friendship prove as strong
To him as his for me.

John Quincy Adams

If you wish to glimpse inside a human soul and get to know a man, don't bother analyzing his ways of being silent, of talking, of weeping, of seeing how much he is moved by noble ideas; you will get better results if you just watch him laugh. If he laughs well, he's a good man.

Fyodor Dostoyevsky

Can the Ham

There's an often-repeated story about a woman who prepares a holiday ham year-after-year. When her daughter is old enough to take an interest in cooking, she watches as her mother prepares the ham. Curious, the little girl asks her mother why she cuts the ends off of the ham before she puts it in the oven. Her mother responds, "Because my mother always did."

The next time the woman visits her mother, she asks her why she always sliced the ends off the holiday ham. "Well," her mother says, "it didn't fit in my pan."

Do you have any proverbial "hams" in your life—things you continue to do, or choose not to do, just because that's what you've always done? Do you refuse to try on clothing with horizontal stripes, because you were told they'd make you look wider? Is there any food you disliked when you were a kid that you've never tried again as an adult? Do you shun joining a friendly game of volleyball, because you were told way-back-when that you're not athletic? How long has it been since you changed your hairstyle? The genre of music you listen to? A long-standing prejudice?

Yes, there's comfort in doing things the same way they've always been done. That's one of the reasons we gravitate toward traditions. During the holidays, we make grandma's special gingerbread recipe. We look forward to reminiscing about the ornaments we've collected over the years as we put them on the tree. But, there's a purpose behind this repetition. It's how we celebrate Christmas. Without the holiday, these repeated rituals lose their meaning.

At this time in our lives, when our mind is already working its hardest just to recall the names of our co-workers, it's tempting to slide into a life of mindless repetition. It's less taxing to continue to do things the way they've always been done. But, if we shrink back from trying something new, we're cutting the sides off of our life and squeezing it into too small of a pan.

Jesus said, "I am come that they might have life, and that they might have it more abundantly" (John 10:10). Abundance is always more than enough. It overflows any vessel that tries to contain it. Thanks to God, we can be so much more than the labels that were put on us as children, stronger than our pesky bad habits, more compassionate than our previously held, small-minded ways of thinking, and more bold and daring than we were when we were young.

Let's not simply settle for becoming older and wiser in the years ahead. Let's push the boundaries of who we were, to become more of who God knows we can be.

Now unto him that is able to do exceeding abundantly
above all that we ask or think,
according to the power that worketh in us,
Unto him be glory in the church by Christ Jesus
throughout all ages, world without end. Amen.

Ephesians 3:20-21

Tradition is a guide, not a jailer.
W. Somerset Maugham

The difficulty lies not so much in developing new
ideas as in escaping from old ones.
John Maynard Keynes

Our second danger is to associate tradition with
the immovable; to think of it as something hostile
to all change; to aim to return to some previous
condition which we imagine as having been
capable of preservation in perpetuity, instead of
aiming to stimulate the life which produced that
condition in its time…a tradition without
intelligence is not worth having.
T. S. Eliot

Tradition is not the worship of ashes,
but the preservation of fire.
Gustav Mahler

There is little success where there is little laughter.
Andrew Carnegie

Family Tradition

The Borgen family had owned the beautiful, lakeside property for generations. During the summer, paddling around the small lake was a favorite family pastime. So, to celebrate her grandson Kevin's eighth birthday, Grandmother Borgen decided to take him out in the family rowboat. They spent the morning happily paddling in and out of secluded coves, as Kevin's grandmother recounted stories of their family's long history in Minnesota.

Starting to get hungry, Grandmother Borgen pointed out a small, tree-lined inlet where they could set up their picnic lunch. She asked Kevin to start rowing that direction. Instead, he stood up, stepped off the side of the boat…and nearly drowned.

"What were you thinking?" the frantic grandmother shouted at her grandson, as she struggled to pull him safely back into the boat.

Wet, shivering, and more than a little embarrassed, Kevin said, "Grandmother, why can't I walk across the lake like you said my father, grandfather, and great-grandfather did on their eighth birthdays?"

"Oh, Kevin," Grandmother Bergen said with a sigh, "They were born in January and you were born in July!"

Just Don't Do It!

A little girl was staying with her Grandmother, Grandmother encouraged her granddaughter to invite the neighbor over to play. When her friend said she needed to use the bathroom, the little girl led her to the one her grandparents used, and then pointed to the scale in the corner. "Whatever you do," cautioned the little girl, "don't step on that thing!"

"Why not?" asked her friend.

"I don't know," replied the little girl, "all I can say is that whenever my grandma gets on it, she starts screaming like mad."

A person without a sense
of humor is like a
wagon without springs
jolted by every pebble in the road.
Henry Ward Beecher

Laughter is the sun
that drives winter
from the human face.
Victor Hugo

The best place to find a helping hand is at the
end of your own arm.
Proverb

It's not what happens to you,
but how you react
to it that matters.
Epictetus

I have not failed.
I've just found 10,000 ways that won't work.
Thomas Edison

We are blind until we see
That in the human plan
Nothing is worth the making
If it does not make the man.

Why build these cities glorious
If man unbuilded goes?
In vain we build the world unless
The Builder also grows.
Edwin Markham

There are no days in life so memorable
as those which vibrated to some stroke
of the imagination.
Ralph Waldo Emerson

Too True

Kim and Wendy, two friends who'd lost contact for many years, bumped into each other unexpectedly one day. Having much to catch up on, Kim commented, "So, I gather from what I've read on social media that you've got your own company now. How wonderful!"

Wendy responded with a shrug of her shoulders, "It's just a small one, nothing to be overly proud of."

"Small?" Kim replied. "I'm sure you're just being modest. How many people work in your company?"

Wendy answered sadly, "About half of them."

You know you're getting older…
when work is a lot of fun—
and fun is a lot of work.

Perchance to Sleep...

Shakespeare wrote, so poetically, "To sleep, perchance to dream…" Of course, his character Hamlet was talking about death. We're just dead on our feet and dreaming of actually falling sleep! You'd think being so exhausted from this busy stage of life would mean we could fall into bed and nod off like a newborn. But, no. We toss. We turn. We kick our blankets off. We pull them back up. We head to the bathroom. Again. We give up, get up, and shop on-line. It's like a nocturnal version of that arcade game where you whack a little rodent-like critter down into a hole, but it just pops up somewhere else, over and over again. That's us.

Unless, of course, we happen to settle in to watch a movie on the couch in the evening. Especially a movie we really want to see. Then, we're snoring before the opening credits are through. But, if we happen to catch ourself nodding off and try to head to our very own bed, well, it's back to tossing and turning. It's enough to drive a mature woman back to the fridge for another bowl of ice cream.

But, considering our current metabolism, which resembles that of an aging sloth, we know that a bedtime snack will only lead to increased frustration when we try and pull on our skinny jeans in the morning. Which are only "skinny" because we no longer are…

What's a bag lady (one who carries them under her eyes) to do? Health experts tell us we can boost our metabolism— by getting more consistent sleep. Talk about a vicious cycle.

We're told cutting back on caffeine may help, but it's the only thing currently allowing us to string coherent sentences together. We can try melatonin, a cup of warm milk (Hey, didn't they have to boil that milk before it was turned into ice cream?), and over the counter sleep aids that leave us feeling so groggy in the morning that we have to up our caffeine intake just to function.

What do we do when nothing works? Often, turning to God—especially for relatively minor frustrations, such as sleeplessness—is our last resort, instead of our first response. We hate to bother God with the trivial stuff. But, God cares about the details. He cares about us.

And God never sleeps. So, when we feel the same is true of us, who better to have a chat with than our Heavenly Father? Whether it's been a matter of hours, or years, since we had a heart-to-heart, He's always ready to listen. We can use those quiet moments to focus on saying "Thank You," to pour out our concerns and frustrations, to pray for those we love, to ask God to help our faith grow, to make us women who make a difference in this world. And if we happen to fall asleep while we're praying, no problem. That may well be God's answer to one of our prayers!

Grown Up
Was it for this I uttered prayers,
And sobbed and cursed and kicked the stairs,
That now, domestic as a plate,
I should retire at half-past eight?

Edna St. Vincent Millay

Early Morning Constitutional
Scotsman Adam Smith was an 18th century
philosopher and economist. He found that when
he was thinking through a problem, going for a
walk would often help. One Sunday morning he
was so deep in thought that he wandered out of
his gate and down the street. Several hours later
he arrived at church, where people were shocked
to see him dressed in his nightgown—
and having walked 15 miles from home.

O Lord, thou knowest how busy I must be this
day. If I forget thee, d
o not thou forget me.

Jacob Astley

My dearest Lord,
be thou a bright flame before me,
be thou a guiding star above me,
be thou a smooth path beneath me,
be though a kindly shepherd behind me,
today—tonight—and forever more.
Columba

Pray, and let God worry.
Martin Luther

I know not by what methods rare,
But this I know: God answers prayer...
I know not if the blessing sought
Will come in just the guise I thought.
I leave my prayer to Him alone
Whose will is wiser than my own.
Eliza M. Hickok

Talk to him in prayer of all your wants, your
troubles, even of the weariness
you feel in serving him. You cannot speak
too freely, too trustfully, of him.

François de la Fénelon

Prayer covers the whole of man's life. There is no
thought, feeling, yearning, or desire however low,
trifling, or vulgar we may deem it, which if it affects
our real interest or happiness, we may not lay before
God and be sure of His sympathy. His nature is such
that our often coming does not tire Him.
The whole burden of the whole life of every man
may be rolled on to God and not weary Him,
though it has wearied the man.

Henry Ward Beecher

Continue in prayer,
and watch in the same with thanksgiving.

Colossians 4:2

Clever Combination

Gail had volunteered to be a substitute Sunday School teacher, but was struggling to open a combination lock on the supply cabinet. She'd been told the combination that morning, but like so many things during this season of her life, she couldn't quite recall what it was.

Since Sunday services hadn't started yet, Gail gave up and headed to the pastor's study to ask for help. Pastor Williams graciously followed her back to the cabinet and began to turn the dial. But, after the first two numbers, he paused, and stared blankly at the lock for a moment. Then, he looked serenely heavenward and his lips began moving silently. When he'd finished, he looked back at the lock, quickly turned the final numbers and opened the lock.

"I'm in awe of your faith, Pastor," Gail said, rather humbled by not having thought to pray first, before bothering the busy pastor.

"It's really nothing," he answered. "We wrote the combination on a piece of tape on the ceiling."

Prayer should be the key of the day
and the lock of the night.
George Herbert

Over The Hill Hymns

Precious Lord, Take My Hand...And Help Me Out of This Recliner

Blessed Insurance

Go Tell It on the Mountain...But Speak Up

Shall We Gather at the Pharmacy

Amazing Gaze...I Found My Reading Glasses!

It Is Well With My Soul...But My Digestion's Not so Hot

Guide Me O Thou Great Jehovah...I've Forgotten Where I Parked

How Firm a Foundation I Require to Jog

This Little Light of Mine...Allows Me to Read the Menu

Just As I Am...With One Bum Knee

Nobody Knows the Trouble I Have Seeing

Count Your Many Birthdays, Name Them One By One

For each new morning with its light,
Father, we thank Thee,
For rest and shelter of the night,
Father, we thank Thee,
For health and food, for love and friends,
For everything Thy goodness sends,
Father in heaven, we thank Thee.

Ralph Waldo Emerson

Prayer does not change God,
but changes him who prays.

Søren Kierkegaard

Prayer is the soul's sincere desire,
Uttered or unexpressed,
The motion of a hidden fire
That trembles in the breast.

James Montgomery

A Touch of Kindness

We all look better in soft focus. Why do you think newscasters and actors, whose careers have lasted well beyond their young adult years, start to look a little fuzzy around the edges onscreen? The right lens. It's why the mirrors in a low-lit bathroom are more flattering than the bright lights of a magnified make-up mirror.

It seems that God, in His infinite wisdom, has given us just the lens we need to welcome in the latter years. It's the one that makes us squint to read a price tag, enlarge the type size on our computer screen, press our nose to the vanity mirror to pluck our eyebrows, and mistakenly believe our shower is perfectly clean—until we happen to see it with our reading glasses on.

Yes, our eyes start to go a bit soft as we age. Perhaps, it's God's way of reminding us that it's about time we learned to view ourselves, and others, in a softer, kinder, more favorable light. Instead of berating ourselves for not fitting into the pants we purchased last year, let's focus on the positive things we've done lately for our body. Maybe we're better friends with vegetables, we're taking a walk on a more regular basis, or we've switched out our diet soda habit for unsweetened ice tea. Maybe we've purchased new pants in a size that actually fits.

If you can't personally think of anything nice you've done for your body lately, perhaps you need more than a change in focus. You need a change of perspective. Consider how you "treat" yourself. How do you celebrate a success? Process a failure? Perk yourself up when you're tired? Calm yourself down when you're angry? If you "treat" your ups and downs pretty much the same way, by overindulging in anything, including sugar, caffeine, shopping, partying, even isolating yourself, you're not really "treating" yourself. You're hurting yourself. And there's nothing loving about that.

"Treating yourself" should mean loving yourself well. That doesn't mean we have to trade in our ice cream for Brussels sprouts. It simply means we're more mindful about the choices we make. If we're sad, ice cream may distract us with sweet creaminess for awhile. But, after we finish the bowl, we'll still be sad. That may lead us back to the carton for yet another fix. Then, chances are we'll not only feel sad, but we'll also feel mad at our lack of self-control. If we really want to treat ourselves, we should deal with the root problem. Our sadness. In the long run, that's the kind, loving thing to do.

Everyone, including each one of us, is fighting some kind of battle each day. And some parts of that battle seem to intensify as we get older. Loving ourselves doesn't mean being hard on ourselves. It means getting real. Yes, we need room to fail and room to grow. We also need perspective, and perseverance, to work toward positive change. Kindness can help. It's like a hug in work clothes.

Kindness is the sunshine in which virtue grows.
Robert G. Ingersoll

123

Sunshine and Shadows

Samuel W. Johnson

Let me live where the sunshine and the shadows merge,
Where the softest light is ever waiting on the verge,
Like a veil to melt away the brightest noonday gleams
And leave sweet fancy to fill the figure of my dreams.
Who would ever want to leave the days that quickly fleet,
Where age and youth in gentle twilight meet,
Where hope and fancy their pearly fretwork weave,
The time before the memories of early childhood leave.
Give me love enough to warm the heart and scent the flower
And weight of gold to drive away the fretful hour;
Just enough of memory to forget the sorrows that are gone,
With rays of hope enduring to kindly lead me on.
Not to know the depths of sadness and surrounding strife;
Not to feel the heat of passion that consumes the better life;
To be within the reach of all that dearest life can give,
Let me between the sunshine and the shadow ever live.

A kind heart is a fountain of gladness,
making everything in its vicinity
freshen into smiles.
Washington Irving

Most folks are about as happy
as they make up their minds to be.
Abraham Lincoln

That best portion of a good man's life—
His little, nameless, unremembered acts
of kindness and of love.
William Wordsworth

A good deed is never lost; he who sows a
courtesy reaps friendship, and he who
plants kindness gathers love.
St. Basil

Treat your friends as you do your pictures,
and place them in their best light.
Jennie Jerome Churchill

I Feel a Breeze

Loretta hadn't been to the Department of Motor Vehicles for many years. She was more than a little anxious, because every time one of her friends had to visit the local office, they complained about what an unpleasant experience it turned out to be. But, Loretta couldn't put it off any longer. Her license was about to expire and it was time for a new photo.

After waiting for quite some time for her number to be called, Loretta was finally next in line. When she got to the counter, the woman in charge handed her a sheet of paper to sign and then barked, "Strip down, facing me."

Loretta was taken aback, but afraid not to comply. So she began to do as instructed. That's when the shouting began—and when Loretta realized the woman had been referring to her credit card.

You know you're getting older when…
you wished you looked as good as the picture
on your driver's license.

Love is blind. Friendship tries not to notice.

Life is most delightful when it is on the
downward slope.
Seneca

One should take good care not to grow too
wise for so great a pleasure of life as laughter.
Joseph Addison

Good humor may be said
to be one of the very best articles
of dress one can wear in society.
William Makepeace Thackeray

Just for the PUN of It!

When two egotists meet, it's an I for an I.

Time flies like an arrow. Fruit flies like a banana.

A chicken crossing the road is poultry in motion.

When a clock is hungry it goes back
for seconds.

He had a photographic memory that was
never developed.

Once you've seen one shopping center,
you've seen a mall.

Adam said to his wife,
"Eve, I wear the plants in the family!"

What happens when seafood tries to dance?
It pulls a mussel.

What do you call someone who used to be called Lee? Formerly.

Two silk worms had a race, but both ended up in a tie.

A gossip is someone with a great sense of rumor.

A sandwich walks into a bar. The bartender says, "We don't serve food here."

A dyslexic man walks into a bra…

An exhausted kangaroo is out of bounds.

How much does it cost for a pirate to get his ears pierced? A buck an ear.

An unlucky man sent ten different puns to a contest, hoping at least one would win. Sadly, no pun in ten did.

The goodness of the true pun is in the
direct ratio of its intolerability.
Edgar Allan Poe

There is one kind of laugh that I always did
recommend; it looks out of the eye first with a
merry twinkle, then it creeps down on its hands
and knees and plays around the mouth like a
pretty moth around the blaze of a candle, then
it steals over into the dimples of the cheeks and
rides around in those whirlpools for a while, then
it lights up the whole face like the mellow bloom
on a damask rose, then it swims up on the air,
with a peal as clear and as happy as a dinner-bell,
then it goes back again on gold tiptoes like an
angel out for an airing, and it lies down on its
little bed of violets in the heart
where it came from.
Josh Billings

We are all here for a spell;
get all the good laughs you can.
Will Rogers

It is a fair, even-handed, noble
adjustment of things, that while there is infection in
disease and sorrow, there is nothing in the world so
irresistibly contagious as laughter
and good-humour.
Charles Dickens

In our play we reveal what kind of
people we are.
Ovid

Men do not quit playing because they grow old; they
grow old because they quit playing.
Oliver Wendell Holmes

Oh, a trouble's a ton, or a trouble's an ounce,
Or a trouble is what you make it,
And it isn't the fact that you're hurt that counts,
But only how did you take it.
Edmund Vance Cooke

Who Are You, Again?

You may be a victim of identity theft. The culprit? Aging. Once upon a time, you may have placed your identity in your good looks. Today, you're still looking good, but people keep adding the phrase "for your age." Or maybe you viewed your primary role in life as being a good mother. Now, the kids are leaving the nest. Yes, you'll always be Mom, but there's a whole new job description. It's now more of an advisory position, much less "hands-on." Unless, of course, you want to be demoted to "meddler." Or, if you've always viewed yourself as "the smart one," you're beginning to feel as though someone's ransacked the filing cabinets of your brain and thrown everything you know out on the floor. Now, anytime you try and retrieve a fact, or sometimes even a word, it's like searching the home of a hoarder to locate one specific sticky-note. And, if you're "the witty one," you're hesitant to even begin telling a joke. You know by the time the punch line roles around, that —just like Elvis—your memory may have left the building…

At this crossroad season in life, who you were, will not always line up with who you are right now. This can leave you feeling aimless and invisible, neither of which inspires anyone to feel much affection for the road that lies ahead. That doesn't mean you're at a dead end. But, it does mean it's time to pause and re-evalaute.

It's like when you turn down a different road than the one your GPS told you to and it needs time to recalculate a new route to your destination. First, it has to figure out where you are. Only then, can it help direct you to where you want to go. Great advice for life, as well as road trips.

Who are you? Really. Your identity is more than the roles you fill, the areas you excel in, or the titles, degrees, or credentials you hold. It's the contours of your heart, your unique personality, life experience, dreams, and desires. It's the fact that you're an individual worthy of love. God makes that very clear. Does that fact redefine how you see yourself?

Perhaps it's time to set aside a day for your own GPS recalculation, using God's Positioning System. Ask Him to help you see yourself clearly, evaluate yourself honestly, and plan new roads for future exploration wisely. Just because you aren't who you were yesterday doesn't mean you can't be someone even more amazing tomorrow.

I find the great thing in the world is not so much where we stand, as in what direction we are moving.

Oliver Wendell Holmes

Use what talents you possess: the woods would
be very silent if no birds sang there
except those that sang best.
Henry Van Dyke

Our deeds still travel with us from afar, and what
we have been makes us what we are.
George Eliot

Every man has in himself a continent
of undiscovered character.
Happy is he who acts as the Columbus
to his own soul.
Sir James Stephen

Far and away the best prize that life offers
is the chance to work hard at work
worth doing.
Theodore Roosevelt

Make the most of yourself,
for that is all there is of you.
Ralph Waldo Emerson

Let every dawn of morning be
to you as the beginning of life
and every setting sun be to you as its close;
then let every one of these
short lives leave its sure record
of some kindly thing done for others,
some goodly strength or knowledge
gained for yourself.

John Ruskin

Did you hear About...

...the rookie police officer who noticed a group of people loitering on a street corner. Wanting to impress his mentor, a senior supervisor on the force, he pulled out his bull horn and yelled, "Everyone, break it up! Go back to your homes immediately!" One by one, the group dispersed, all looking puzzled, and many downright frightened. "So how did I do?" the officer asked his supervisor. "Not bad," the veteran officer replied, "considering this is a bus stop."

If you can laugh at yourself,
you'll never run out of
things to laugh at.

It's never too late to
have a happy childhood.

Ruin the day for a grouch:
smile!

Imagination was given to man
to compensate him for what he
is not; a sense of humor
to console him for what he is.

Francis Bacon

Do all the good you can,
By all the means you can,
In all the ways you can,
In all the places you can,
At all the times you can,
To all the people you can,
As long as ever you can.

John Wesley

To make a sunrise in a place
Where darkness reigned alone;
To light new gladness in a face
That joy has never known;
To plant a little happiness
In plots where weeds run riot—
Takes very little time, and oh,
It isn't hard—just try it!

Author Unknown

Easy Rider

When Sandra got off work, she walked outside into a downpour. With no coat, hat, or umbrella, she dreaded the half hour walk uphill all the way home. Just then, a car pulls up right next to the curb. Thinking it's a friend, or a stranger who's taken pity on her plight, Sandra gets in and turns to the driver to say, "Thank you." But, no one's there. She's alone in the car. Before she can respond, the car slowly starts moving forward, without a sound.

For the next two miles, the car continues straight ahead, stopping at every light and obeying all of the traffic laws. Spellbound—and thankful to remain dry—Sandra stays seated in silence, until the car eventually comes to a complete stop at the top of the hill where she lives. She gets out, closes the door and turns around to head up her walk, when she almost bumps into another guy who's trying to get into the car.

"Hey," she says to him, holding her purse over her head to protect her hair from the rain. "I'm not sure I'd get in there if I were you. There's something weird going on!"

"Yeah, I know," the guy replies. "But I just pushed my car three miles and I can use a rest going down the hill."

> Just remember, once you're over the hill
> you begin to pick up speed.
> Arthur Schopenhauer

The Joyful Journey

Regardless of our current age, one thing holds true: today is the youngest we'll ever be for the rest of our life. Instead of mourning youthful days gone by, let's celebrate the slice of youth and vitality God's serving up to us today. Then, tomorrow, let's do it all over again!

That, my friend, is the secret of living a joy-filled life. It begins by being aware of the blessings within our grasp at this very moment. For some of us, this may be a habit we need to acquire. If so, spend a few minutes each morning asking God to open your eyes to the little wellsprings of joy that are yours today. Perhaps it begins with the warm cup of coffee you're sipping from your favorite mug. Maybe it includes hearing the voices of your children getting ready in the morning—even if they're fighting over whose turn it is to use the bathroom. It might even be the fact that you're wearing your favorite shoes, the red ones that always make you smile. Then, in the evening before you go to bed, once again spend a few moments with God. Thank Him for every blessing He's brought to mind.

These few moments of prayer and praise help prime the pump of our hearts with a trickle of gratitude. The more it becomes part of our daily routine, the more that trickle grows. Soon, it overflows into every area of our lives. That's when we notice that our fears and frustrations with growing older begin to take a backseat to experiencing the beauty and wonder of where we are right now on this journey of life. It's true that we'll never be this age again. We'll never see the world, or ourselves, through exactly the same eyes as we do today. So, let's savor this moment, right here and right now.

Regardless of our circumstances, whether we're sailing through our current season with ease or struggling to navigate the stormy seas of heartache and change, there's always reason to give thanks. When we do, we'll discover that gratitude's constant companion is joy—and that joy will become our companion as well. It will keep us young as we grow old, ready to welcome the future with open arms and a hopeful heart.

Strength and honour are her clothing;
and she shall rejoice in time to come.
Proverbs 31:25

To live content with small means;
to seek elegance rather than luxury,
and refinement rather than fashion;
to be worthy, not respectable,
and wealthy, not rich;
to study hard, think quietly,
talk gently, act frankly;
to listen to the stars and birds,
to babes and sages, with open heart;
to bear all cheerfully, do all bravely,
await occasions, hurry never.
In a word to let the spiritual,
unbidden and unconscious,
grow up through the common.
This is to be my symphony.

William Henry Channing

Write it on your heart that every day
is the best day in the year.
Ralph Waldo Emerson

It is not how old you are,
but how you are old.
Jules Renard

The most completely lost
of all days is that on
which one has not laughed.
Nicolas Chamfort

I send you my best wishes for a happy New Year...
in which you will have pleasure in
living every day,
without waiting for the days to be gone
before finding charm in them,
and without putting all hope of pleasure
in the days to come.
Marie Curie

May you live all the days of your life.
Jonathan Swift